NOLEY 1/13

EXPLORERS!

Vasco Núñez de Balboa

Explorer to the Pacific Ocean

Arlene Bourgeois Molzahn

Enslow Publishers, Inc.

40 Industrial Road	PO Box 38
Box 398	Aldershot
Berkeley Heights, NJ 07922	Hants GU12 6BP
USA	UK

http://www.enslow.com

To my grandson, Joey, who has a kind and loving heart
and whose visits always bring me so much joy.

Library of Congress Cataloging-in-Publication Data

Molzahn, Arlene Bourgeois.
    Vasco Núñez de Balboa: explorer to the Pacific Ocean / Arlene Bourgeois Molzahn.
        p. cm. — (Explorers!)
    Summary: Discusses the life of Vasco Núñez de Balboa, with an emphasis on his explorations and his crossing of
the Isthmus of Panama.
    Includes bibliographical references (p.   ) and index.
    ISBN 0-7660-2142-4
    1. Balboa, Vasco Núñez de, 1475-1519—Juvenile literature. 2. Explorers—America—Biography—Juvenile litera-
ture. 3. Explorers—Spain—Biography—Juvenile literature. 4. America—Discovery and exploration—Spanish—
Juvenile literature. 5. Pacific Ocean—Discovery and exploration—Spanish—Juvenile literature. [1. Balboa, Vasco
Núñez de, 1475-1519. 2. Explorers. 3. America—Discovery and exploration—Spanish.] I. Title. II. Explorers!
(Enslow Publishers)
E125.B2M65 2003
973.1'6'092—dc21   2002155205

Printed in the United States of America

10 9 8 7 6 5 4 3 2 1

To Our Readers: We have done our best to make sure all Internet Addresses in this book were active and appropri-
ate when we went to press. However, the author and the publisher have no control over and assume no liability for
the material available on those Internet sites or on other Web sites they may link to. Any comments or suggestions
can be sent by e-mail to comments@enslow.com or to the address on the back cover.

Every effort has been made to locate all copyright holders of material used in this book. If any errors or omissions
have occurred, corrections will be made in future editions of this book.

Illustration Credits: © 1996-2003 ArtToday.com, Inc., p. 38, 41; © 1999 Artville, LLC., pp. 4, 8
(map), 19, 23; Corel Corporation, pp. 13, 30, 33; Library of Congress, pp. 1, 6, 7, 8 (portrait), 10, 11
(all), 12, 16 (all), 18, 20, 22, 24, 25, 26, 28, 29, 31, 32, 36, 37, 39.

Cover Illustration: background, Monster Zero Media; portrait, Library of Congress.

Please note: Compasses on the cover and in the book are from © 1999 Artville, LLC.

Contents

List of Maps

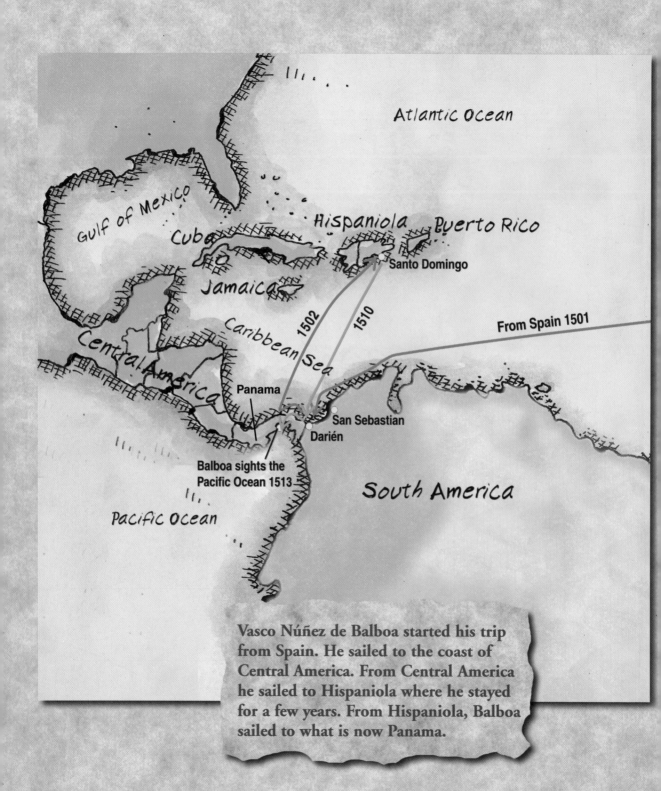

Vasco Núñez de Balboa started his trip from Spain. He sailed to the coast of Central America. From Central America he sailed to Hispaniola where he stayed for a few years. From Hispaniola, Balboa sailed to what is now Panama.

Escape from Hispaniola

In 1501, Vasco Núñez de Balboa sailed from Spain with Rodrigo de Bastidas and his crew. They were searching for riches in lands that had just been discovered. They sailed from Spain and reached the coast of Central America. The explorers traded goods with the people who lived there.

The explorers were soon ready to return to Spain with the riches they gathered. But they discovered sea worms had damaged their ships. The sea worms ate the wood of their ships and caused the ships to leak. The leaky ships had to stop for repairs at some nearby islands. Thinking they had fixed their ships, the men set off for Spain.

To escape from Hispaniola, Balboa hid in a barrel to sneak onto a ship in 1510.

The sea worms had done more damage than the men thought. The explorers almost did not make it to the island of Hispaniola. The ships sank off the coast. Today, Hispaniola is made up of two countries, Haiti and the Dominican Republic.

Luckily, the men were able to get ashore with most of the riches. Bastidas eventually sailed back to Spain.

Balboa stayed in Hispaniola. He raised pigs and farmed a small piece of land but did not make any money. He wanted to explore the lands he had seen while sailing with Bastidas. But he could not leave Hispaniola because his farm left him with no money. The law said that people could not leave the island without first paying all their bills.

One day, in 1510, Balboa decided to leave. He hid on a ship. Some say he wrapped himself in a sail. Others say he hid in a barrel.

Once the ship was out to sea, Balboa came out of his hiding place. The captain of the ship was Martín Fernández de Enciso. He was mad when he saw Balboa, but he let Balboa stay. Balboa became a part of the crew. They were on the way to South America.

When the ship was out to sea, Balboa came out of the barrel and joined the crew.

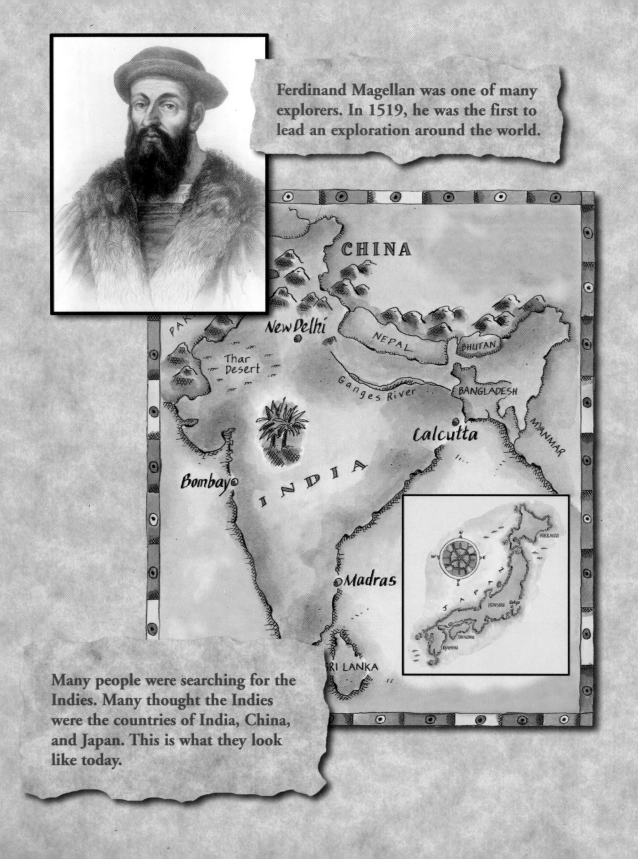

Ferdinand Magellan was one of many explorers. In 1519, he was the first to lead an exploration around the world.

Many people were searching for the Indies. Many thought the Indies were the countries of India, China, and Japan. This is what they look like today.

The Age of Exploration

The 1400s were the beginning of the Age of Exploration. In Europe, many men were searching for a faster route to the Indies. They sailed the oceans looking for spices, gold, and other riches. Earlier in history, some people thought the world was flat. But by the 1500s, most thought the world was round. Although, some sailors did think there were sea monsters hiding in the oceans.

Crossing the great sea was a dream for many. Two famous explorers of this time were Christopher Columbus and Ferdinand Magellan. Each explorer had his own idea about searching for treasure and discovering new lands.

Christopher Columbus discovered new lands as he was trying to find the Indies.

Christopher Columbus (1451-1506)

Christopher Columbus was born in Genoa, Italy. Like many explorers of his time, he wanted to find an all-water route to the Indies. Columbus thought if he sailed west he would find the Indies. He actually landed on islands in the Caribbean Sea, which he thought were the Indies. Columbus went on four trips between 1492 and 1504. During these four trips, he explored what are today called the West Indies and the coasts of Central and South America.

Vasco Núñez de Balboa heard about the lands, people, and riches that Columbus had found. Sailors returning from these new lands told wonderful stories. Balboa was excited and ready to explore. He wanted to get rich and become famous.

Vasco Núñez de Balboa was born about 1475. He was born in Jerez de los Caballeros, Spain. His father was Nuño Arias de Balboa. Vasco had three brothers, Alvar, Gonzalo, and Juan.

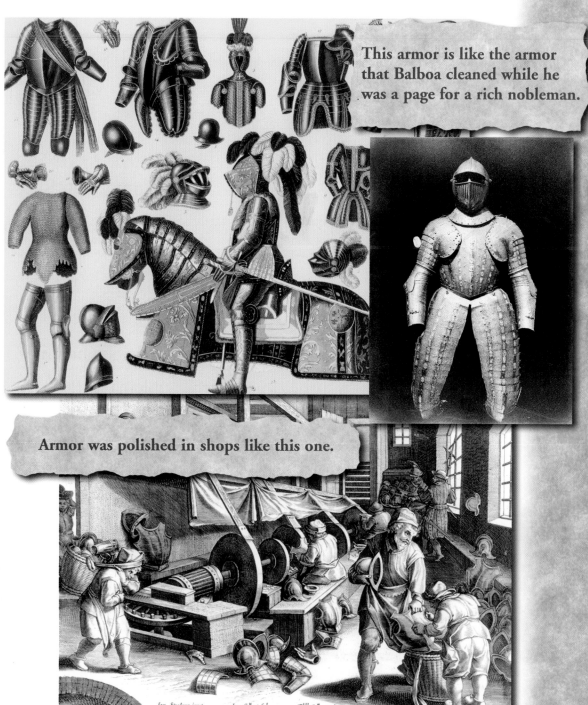

This armor is like the armor that Balboa cleaned while he was a page for a rich nobleman.

Armor was polished in shops like this one.

Christopher Columbus shared stories of his discoveries with the king and queen of Spain.

The Balboa family could trace their history back to the royal house of Spain. At one time, the family had been rich and important. But by 1475, the family had very little money and was no longer important.

At a very young age, Balboa became a page for a rich nobleman. Balboa lived with the nobleman's family in the port city of Moguer, Spain. He had many different jobs as a page. He kept the knight's armor shining. He kept the knight's other clothes clean and ready for the knight to wear. Balboa helped the knight dress and helped him get on his horse. Serving meals to the knight and his guests was also part of his job.

Balboa also had to do many other jobs. In return for

Balboa was not happy living in the quiet Spanish countryside. He wanted the adventure and excitement of the famous explorers, like Columbus.

Haiti Today

Haiti is a country in the West Indies. It is part of the island of Hispaniola. The other side of the island is the Dominican Republic. Haiti's capital is Port-au-Prince. Most people who live on Haiti are farmers. They raise beans, corn, rice, and yams. In the valleys and on the mountains of Haiti, people grow coffee, cacao (the bean used to make chocolate), and sugar cane.

his work, Balboa learned to read and write. He was also taught how to hunt and how to ride a horse.

Balboa was not very happy working as a page. He wanted to go to battle or sail the seas. Every day Balboa watched as captains got their ships ready to sail across the great ocean. He watched as other ships came into Moguer loaded with treasures. Balboa would soon get his chance to sail. Now twenty-six years old, Balboa heard of Rodrigo de Bastidas.

In 1500, Rodrigo de Bastidas talked with King Ferdinand and Queen Isabella of Spain. They told

Bastidas he could explore all the islands and lands that had not already been claimed by Spain. He was given the right to take all the gold, silver, and riches of any kind that he found. He was to bring them back to Spain. One fourth of all he brought back would belong to the king. The rest would be his.

So in 1501, Balboa had joined Bastidas and his crew as they sailed across the ocean. They sailed to the coast of Central America and Hispaniola. It was on Hispaniola that Balboa had a farm. In 1510, left with no money to pay his bills, he hid on a ship and escaped.

Dominican Republic Today

The Dominican Republic is a country in the West Indies. It is part of the island of Hispaniola. The other side of the island is Haiti. Santo Domingo is the capital of the Dominican Republic. There are many mountains in the Dominican Republic. Most people who live in rural areas are farmers. People who live in the cities work in factories, for the government, or by fishing.

The Indians did not want the Spaniards to take their gold and take over their land.

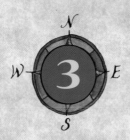

San Sebastian

After his escape from Hispaniola, Vasco Núñez de Balboa was now a part of Enciso's crew. They were sailing to help Alonso de Ojeda. Ojeda had hoped to find gold. The soldiers on Ojeda's ships attacked many Indian villages along the northern coast of South America. They searched the villages and took all the gold they could find. They also took many men as slaves. But as the Spaniards searched for gold, the Indians attacked them. They killed many Spaniards.

Ojeda made it back to his ship, and ordered all three ships to start sailing west. Enciso sailed back to

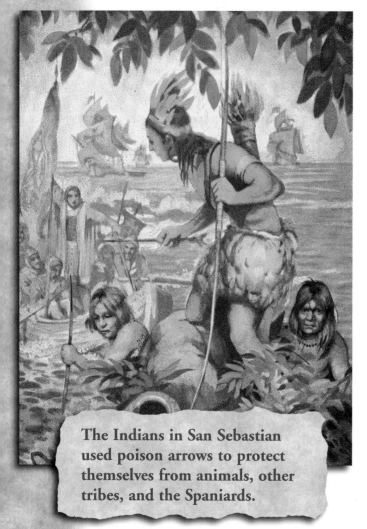

The Indians in San Sebastian used poison arrows to protect themselves from animals, other tribes, and the Spaniards.

Hispaniola instead. Ojeda and his ships came to a small gulf along the coast of what today is Colombia. Ojeda had his men build a settlement there. He named the settlement San Sebastian.

The Spaniards had a hard time in San Sebastian. The Indians who lived there used poison on their arrows. This protected them from dangerous animals and other tribes. They also used their arrows on the Spaniards. People died soon after being hit by these poison arrows. Whenever the Spaniards tried to hunt for food they were shot with arrows. The men also became sick with yellow fever. Men were dying every day from

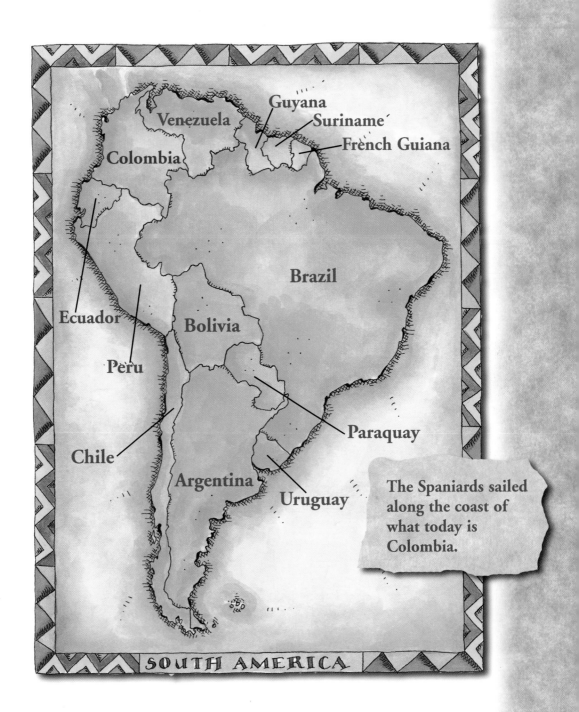

Venezuela
Guyana
Suriname
French Guiana
Colombia

Brazil

Ecuador
Bolivia

Peru

Paraquay

Chile

Argentina
Uruguay

The Spaniards sailed along the coast of what today is Colombia.

SOUTH AMERICA

sickness, hunger, or the poison arrows. One day, Ojeda took a ship and left for Hispaniola to get help.

When Ojeda reached Hispaniola, he got Enciso to sail back with a large group of soldiers. He wanted them to help the men he had left at San Sebastian. Among Enciso's crew was Vasco Núñez de Balboa.

The Spaniards had to leave San Sabastian and sail to Hispaniola to get help.

A New Leader

Trouble followed the Spaniards. On the way to San Sebastian, one of Enciso's ships sank. The men were saved but the food and horses that the ship carried were lost.

The ships reached San Sebastian and rescued the men who had been left there. All the buildings had been burned to the ground. Almost every time the Spaniards went ashore, they were attacked by the Indians who lived there. The food supply became very low. It was not safe for the Spaniards to search for food on land.

Enciso did not know what to do. He asked each man

what should be done. Almost everyone wanted to leave San Sebastian. There was not enough room on the ship to take all the men back to Hispaniola.

Then Balboa told the men what he remembered from his travels with Bastidas. He said he knew of a place where the land was good and there was plenty of food. A large river flowed through the land. There were friendly villages. He said that they all should sail there. The men thought Balboa's plan was a good one.

Balboa led his men to a village. They named it Santa María de la Antigua del Darién.

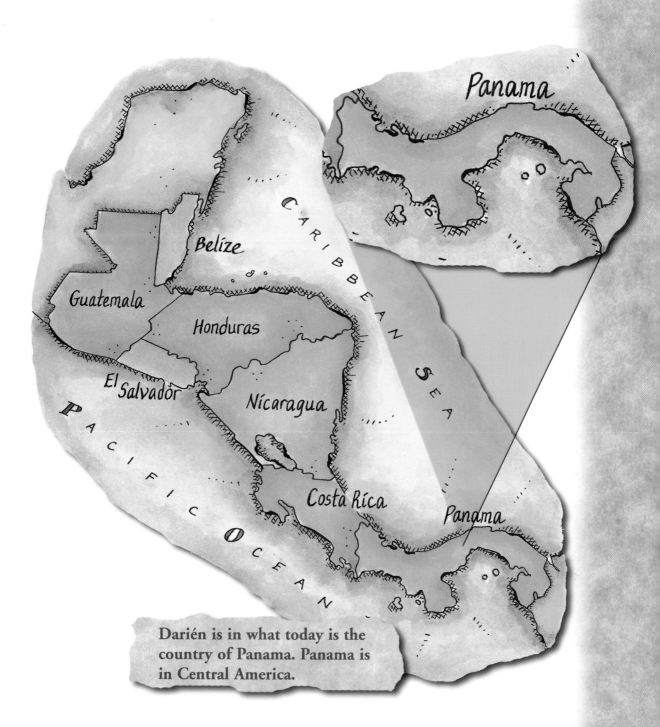

Panama

Belize

Guatemala

Honduras

El Salvador

Nicaragua

Costa Rica

Panama

C A R I B B E A N   S E A

P A C I F I C   O C E A N

Darién is in what today is the
country of Panama. Panama is
in Central America.

Balboa's men found many types of new food, such as coconuts, on the land Balboa told them about.

The Spaniards found the land just as Balboa had told them. The men found many new types of food. They ate potatoes, corn, and pineapples. They also made flour from the root of the cassava plant. This flour was used to make bread. The men also found that the Indians had a lot of gold. The men settled in the village and named it Santa María de la Antigua del Darién. They called it Darién for short. This village was in what today is the country of Panama in Central America.

Enciso, as captain of the ship, was in charge of the Spaniards in Darién. One day he made a law that he was the only person who could trade gold with the people. No one else could trade goods for gold. Any man found keeping gold for himself would be put to death.

The men were angry. They felt that Enciso was being very unfair. They decided to vote for a new leader. They chose Vasco Núñez de Balboa.

Soon other ships brought Spanish settlers to Darién. Enciso and a few of his followers returned to Spain. After they left, Balboa was in charge of the settlement at Darién.

Once the men were settled in Darién, Enciso decided he wanted all the gold for himself. He made a law that no one else could trade with the Indians for gold.

When Balboa heard about lands around Darién, he went in search of them.

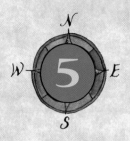

Reaching the
South Sea

Balboa and his men left Darién and began exploring Panama. They captured several villages. They traded bells and shiny glass beads for gold.

One day, Balboa was told about a river valley that was full of gold. He was very interested in finding that valley.

Balboa was also told about an unending sea that was over the mountains. He learned all about the lands that had to be crossed. Soon Balboa gathered supplies for a trip to reach this great body of water.

On September 1, 1513, Balboa left Darién to search for the great unending sea. He took 190 Spanish soldiers

and 800 Indians with him. They had to cross the Isthmus of Panama. An isthmus is a narrow strip of land separating two bodies of water. It also connects two larger areas of land. The Isthmus of Panama separates the Atlantic Ocean from the Pacific Ocean. It also connects North America and South America.

Balboa and his men fought and captured many Indians as they crossed the Isthmus of Panama.

The Indians were forced to become guides for Balboa and his men.

The men soon came to many huge swamps as they traveled over land. These swamps were filled with poisonous snakes, crocodiles, and mosquitoes. After the swamps, the men had to cut their way through jungles. Later, they had to climb high mountains.

Balboa and his men reached many villages as they

One day, Balboa and his men climbed a mountain and looked below. They saw water as far as they could see.

After finding the ocean, Balboa had a cross built and set up on the shore. He then claimed the ocean for the king and queen of Spain.

climbed the mountains. The Spaniards quickly captured these villages. At each village, the Spaniards stole gold.

Some of the Indians were forced to become guides for Balboa. These people knew the area well.

Then one day, Balboa climbed a mountain peak and

Balboa was the first European man to see this ocean.

looked down below. There, for as far as he could see, was water. Balboa called it Mar del Sur (South Sea). Today that body of water is called the Pacific Ocean. Explorer Ferdinand Magellan actually named the Pacific Ocean in 1520.

Balboa quickly fell to his knees. He was thankful that God had let him be the first European man to see this ocean. His men built an altar with rocks and placed a cross in the middle of it. Then the men began to climb down the mountain toward the ocean.

Balboa may have been the first European to see the Pacific Ocean, but it was Ferdinand Magellan who named the ocean.

On September 29, 1513, they reached the Pacific Ocean. The men tasted the salty water, and they cut their initials into the trees along the shore. Balboa claimed the ocean for the king and queen of Spain.

The gold the explorers had stolen from the villages was very heavy to carry. Their food supplies were getting low. So Balboa and all his men returned to Darién.

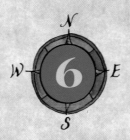

Treason and Trial

When he reached Darién, Balboa wrote a report to the king. He told him about the Pacific Ocean and about the riches he had gathered for Spain.

In April 1514, a ship arrived in Darién from Spain. It quickly unloaded its cargo and returned. A friend took Balboa's letter back to Spain on that ship.

By the end of June 1514, twenty-two ships from Spain had arrived at Darién. The ships had left Spain before Balboa's letter reached King Ferdinand. A man named Pedrarias Dávila was on one of the ships. The king had named him governor of Darién.

Darién became a popular place for the Spaniards. Ships arrived with many people.

Finally, a letter arrived from King Ferdinand. The king had heard of Balboa's discovery of the Pacific Ocean. He made Balboa an admiral. He also named him governor of the Pacific Ocean and of all the lands that he discovered. This made Dávila very unhappy.

Balboa continued to explore the land along the Pacific Ocean. He wrote in his journal that it would be a good idea to cut a channel through this land.

Many centuries later the United States did. The Panama Canal cuts across the Isthmus of Panama. It is a shorter route for ships. Before the canal was built, ships sailed around the southern tip of South America.

Balboa was arrested and thrown in jail because Pedrarias Dávila was jealous of the land and riches Balboa had found.

Panama Canal

The Panama Canal is a waterway that cuts across the Isthmus of Panama. It links the Atlantic Ocean and the Pacific Ocean. Before the canal was built, ships had to travel around the tip of South America. A ship going from New York City to San Francisco, California, traveled about 13,000 miles. After the canal was built, the trip took less than 5,200 miles.

The canal was started in the early 1900s and was finished in 1914. Thousands of people worked on the canal. They cut through jungles and swamps while battling diseases caused by mosquitoes.

How Does a Ship Get From the Atlantic to the Pacific?

A ship going from the Atlantic Ocean to the Pacific Ocean enters the canal from Limón Bay. The ship heads toward the Gatún Locks. There, the ship is raised by three water-filled chambers called locks. Locks raise and lower the ship from one level to another.

Once the ship passes through the three locks, it enters Gatún Lake. It sails across the lake to Gaillard Cut. The cut is a manmade passageway. Gaillard Cut takes the ship to the Pedro Miguel Locks. The ship is lowered into Miraflores Lake. It sails across the lake to the Miraflores Locks. From these locks, the ship heads into the Bay of Panama and then the Pacific Ocean. The whole trip takes about eight hours.

Without the Panama Canal, ships would have to sail around South America. The canal lets ships travel between the Atlantic and Pacific Oceans.

Balboa and his men returned to Darién. Dávila did not like Balboa. He was jealous of all the land and riches Balboa had found. He sent men to arrest Balboa. Balboa was put in jail and charged with treason. Treason is the betraying of one's country by helping an enemy.

Dávila claimed that Balboa wanted to start a country separate from Spain. A quick and unfair trial was held, and it was decided that Balboa would die. On January 20, 1519, Vasco Núñez de Balboa was put to death in Acla, Panama.

Vasco Núñez de Balboa was put to death after a quick and unfair trial.

Balboa Park

In San Diego, California, there is a park called Balboa Park. This park was once called City Park, but in 1910 a contest was held to rename it. The name chosen was Balboa Park because Vasco Núñez de Balboa was the first European to see the Pacific. The park also offers a wide view of the Pacific Ocean. Balboa Park has many museums, theaters, and gardens. It is home to the San Diego Zoo.

Vasco Núñez de Balboa was a great Spanish explorer. He crossed the Isthmus of Panama. He was the first European man to see the eastern part of the Pacific Ocean. Balboa opened the door for Spanish exploration on the west coast of South America.

Timeline

1475—Vasco Núñez de Balboa is born probably in the city of Jerez de los Caballeros, Spain.

1501—Sails with Rodrigo de Bastidas.

1502—Lands on the island of Hispaniola; Balboa stays and raises pigs.

1510—Hides on a ship and reaches San Sebastian; Left in charge of Darién.

September 1, 1513—Leaves Darién to search for the Pacific Ocean.

September 29, 1513—Crosses the Isthmus of Panama; Discovers the Pacific Ocean.

June 1514—Pedrarias Dávila, the new governor of Darién, arrives.

1518—Dávila arrests Balboa.

January 20, 1519—Vasco Núñez de Balboa is beheaded in Acla, Panama, after unjustly being accused of treason.

Words to Know

admiral—A commander in charge of a navy.

cargo—Goods carried by ships, planes, trucks, or vehicles.

cassava—A plant grown in warm lands in the Americas. The roots are used to make tapioca, are eaten like potatoes, or are ground into flour.

channel—A body of water that connects two larger bodies of water.

exploration—The act of exploring.

governor—A person who is elected or appointed ruler of a certain area.

gulf—A part of an ocean or sea stretching out into the land.

nobleman—A man of very high rank.

port—A place where ships can load and unload.

route—A way people traveled, like a road.

settlement—A place that is newly settled; a small village.

swamp—Wet land often partly covered by water.

trial—Studying the facts as a way to prove something is true or false.

valley—Lowland between mountains or hills.

village—A place where people live that is smaller than a town.

yellow fever—A disease spread by mosquitoes in hot countries.

Learn More About
Vasco Núñez de Balboa

Books

Marcovitz, Hal. *Vasco Nunez de Balboa and the Discovery of the South Sea*. Broomall, Penn.: Chelsea House Publishers, 2001.

Prevost, John F. *Pacific Ocean*. Minneapolis, Minn.: ABDO Publishing Company, 2000.

Winkelman, Barbara G. *The Panama Canal*. Danbury, Conn.: Children's Press, 1999.

Learn More About
Vasco Núñez de Balboa

Internet Addresses

The Panama Canal: Photo Gallery

<http://www.pancanal.com/eng/photo/index.html>

See photos from the past and present of the Panama Canal.

Vasco Nunez de Balboa: Spanish Conquistador and Explorer

<http://www.enchantedlearning.com/explorers/page/b/

balboa.shtml>

Check out this Web site from Enchanted Learning.

Index